The Beaten Face

By: Demeteria Adams Kossie

Edited by: Kaylee Overbey

Royal Media Publishing

Jeffersonville, IN

Royal Media and Publishing
P. O. Box 4321
Jeffersonville, IN 47131
502-802-5385
http://royamediaandpublishing.com
royalmediapublishing@gmail.com

© Copyright – 2015

All Rights Reserved. No part of this book may be reproduced, stored in a retrieval system, or transmitted by any means without the written permission of the author.

Published by: Royal Media Publishing
Cover photo: Image Source
Layout: Royal Media Publishing

ISBN 13: 978-0692573624
ISBN-10: 0692573623

Printed in the United States of America

Acknowledgements

I would like to thank my Mother, Ada Adams for being the trooper she is and allowing me to share her story. Mama has always given me good advice on life and relationships. I would like to thank three very important ladies in my life, that either helped to jump start me or keep pushing me forward. First, my daughter, Ms. Cierra Adams, my Rockstar, best friend, Mrs. Claire Peters, and last, my good friend who drove a 100 miles to type my book, Mrs. Tracee Jordan.

I LOVE YOU ALL

Table of Contents

Acknowledgements
    Chapter 1   1

    Chapter 2   17

    Chapter 3   33

    Chapter 4   47

    Chapter 5   53

    Chapter 6   59

Resources   66
About the Author   67

Chapter 1

How It All Started

In the big city people can hide things. In big cities, people can go unnoticed and unacknowledged for months. People in big cities don't ask too many questions, or even speak to each other for that matter. Houston, Texas is one of those huge cities that can hide a lot of things-- like people and their personalities. Our family was fine in the big city. My mama was raised in a good family, the family wasn't perfect but they were all taken care of and safe.

When you are growing up in a good family with a wonderful mother and a good step-father, what would make you settle for less? My mama's stepfather was not your typical stepfather. He treated her like a queen as if she were his very own flesh and blood. He never laid an inappropriate hand on my mama, her mother or any of her sisters and brothers.

Because of the treatment by my mother's stepfather, my mother was looking for someone to keep a promise, a promise to love and take care of her and any children that she bore. There is something about love and promises that makes you do things that you never thought you would. You stand before a preacher and promise to love, honor and cherish. You promise that you will love, work hard and look after each other until the day you die. Back then, a man approached you with a hat in his hand, laying on his chest which was a sign of his promise. You promise before God and man that you will, but will you really? Some people make promises that they keep and those promises bring pain. The promises that bring pain are long lasting and can be the most damaging.

Moving to the country was the worst thing my mama could have done. Independence, Texas is a small, country town west of Houston, Texas. There is nothing in Independence but country roads, oak trees as well as lots of farms and animals. Most of the houses the people live in look like old shacks or are old and boarded up. There are maybe four or five houses that are well built by people who own many acres of land. There is only one small store called Mickey's and it is family owned by loving people that care for everyone, but once the store closes at 6 o'clock you have to travel to the next town which is 13 miles away.

Momma was pretty with smooth, dark skin and a slender build. When Mama smiled she had four gold teeth that would shine so pretty against her brown skin. Mama wore wigs all the time, her wig of choice was an extra-large puffy wig with the big curls and her wig always had to be jet black. Along with her wig, she also loved to wear stretch jump suits, and these were the jump suits that hugged your shape and showed your curves in all of the right places.

Mama loved to mingle with everyone that she would meet. She was a loving, outspoken woman that would make friends with anyone of any race. Momma was so kind, she was known for her willingness to give a stranger the shirt off her back. That's just the kind of warm, loving heart my mama had, because of her looks and personality mama never had trouble attracting a man. Her only problem was getting the right man.

On a cold, late December night, the glare from the light of the Christmas tree shines throughout the house. Everyone was asleep except mama. She was up cleaning and decorating the house for Christmas while Christmas music played in the background. The decorations were minimal but colorful all the same, there was small tree, some candles and the smell of fruit was in the air.

In the midst of the Christmas cheer, we heard the moans and groans of a drunkard. There were repeated loud knocks at the door, and a voice that was saying "hold on man, stop!" Mama opened the front door and there stood Jay. Jay was her man and he was standing there drunk as a skunk. He was so drunk that he fell through the door, stumbled to the couch and then passed out.

Mama, would tell Jay's friend Ike that she was tired of Jay getting drunk and that she was tired of putting up with the mess of a drunk. Ike would tell her to get rid of Jay and let him move in but mama would only laugh and Ike would continually tell her that he was the man for her. Ike bragged about what he could do for her and she would always say to him, "you and Lilly are my friends I wouldn't dare do her like that." Lilly was Ike's girlfriend at the time.

Ike's skin was very bright and light in complexion for a black man. Ike was so light skinned that some people thought he was white. He had big, beautiful, eyes the color of ocean water and his teeth were as white as snow. He was very handsome and to some women, like mama, he was irresistible.

    Every chance Ike got he would make a pass at momma. Sometimes Ike would purposely get Jay drunk so he could make a pass at momma. Over the next few weeks after Christmas, there were several instances of Jay getting drunk. He would come home and want to fight with mama but she told him that she was tired of his mess and that she had had enough. She then asked him to leave and go back to Houston to live with his parents. Jay insisted that he wasn't going anywhere but Ike was there as well and he told momma that he would take Jay home with him until the next day. Jay didn't want to leave without a fight, but mom told Ike that he better take him on before she called the cops. Ike left with Jay, but mysteriously, Ike later returned by himself.

Mama told him that he needed to get going because it was late and she was ready for bed. Then, Ike decided to make his move by telling her how much he liked her and that he had liked her for a long time. He told her that Jay was not the man for her and he promised that he would help her and her kids.

Mama once again asked about Lilly saying, "What about Lilly, she's my friend and I can't do her like that."

But Ike with his smooth silky voice would say, "Lilly doesn't really like you, she's always telling me that and I think that she and Jay had a fling with each other." He then continued by saying "Lilly ain't my woman she's just a friend. I wanna make you my woman. Damn what the people say or think. So whatcha gonna do?"

Ike's smooth words made momma think and blush. Mama was tired of Jay's mess and what Ike was saying was making some sense but mama was still hesitant.

Mama said, "I don't know Ike, that's going to be a lot of mess when Jay and Lilly find out."

"To hell with them!" Ike yelled out. "Do you want a good man or not?"

Mama said, "Yea I do want a good man, but I don't have time for drama."

Wasting no time, Ike said, "I'm moving in tomorrow! I'll make sure Jay gets on that greyhound first thing in the morning and as far as Lilly goes you don't have to worry about her, she won't be coming back either."

So when morning came, Ike put Jay on the greyhound, then he made his final stop before coming to live with mama. Ike brought all of his belongings along with his lies that were enveloped in promises and hidden by secrets of the monster he was but it didn't take long for that monster to come out. By the weekend, mama would be introduced to the monster.

Every Friday night mama and her friends would go to the hole in the wall, a well-known club downtown. Ike came home from work looking for mama. He found out that mama was out clubbing and oh, that made him mad. He came to the club and snatched her out of the front door, cursing and pushing on her. He was pulling one way, and she was pulling another which only made him madder. Seemingly out of nowhere, he slapped mama, she was stunned and they began to fight. They fought all the way home, they fought hard and they had only had been together for one week.

The next morning mama woke up to her first swollen face and Ike began his first of many crying spells. Ike apologies to her and says how sorry he was. He would say, "Please forgive me," and mama would fall for it every time. She would give him another chance and she would say, "it only happened cause he jealous." Somehow Ike's jealousy made mama feel like something special or 'super woman.' Even though mama tried to take Ike's jealous actions as a reverse compliment, there was nothing nice or flattering about his actions. The beatings seemed to happen more often and mama began to stay away from family and friends.

Six months passed and things got worse, Ike's temper really got out of hand. By this time, mama was expecting a child due in late September, but Ike was not happy at all. Ike not only took his anger out on mama but also on the other children that mama already had. He started being mean to my sister and brother and would not allow them to go outside and play. Ike expected them to do hard chores until he said to stop. He dared momma to talk against treatment of the children and his harsh rules. Sometimes he would make them work until the sun came up and he would threaten either of them to be asleep when they were supposed to be working. Many times they would talk about running away, but where would they have gone? They talked about how much they hated Ike while they worked. Neither of them like how much mama had changed since she had been with Ike. Mama let Ike treat them any way he liked, and they just couldn't believe her behavior. She was letting him do them this way, letting him take over the house and control her. They wished for their daddy Jay to come back home but it seemed like that was never going to happen.

Nine months went by and on September 26 at 8 o'clock in the morning I was born, weighing in at only 5lbs 8 oz. Momma said that Ike seemed to be happy after I was born. Momma thought that Ike was happy with the baby and the move back to the country, but not so. After we made the move back to the country to the small community of

Independence, Texas, that's when it all went from bad to even worse. Ike got his wish and mama did as she was told. Mama agreed to leave her nice, warm apartment in town to move into a small, old shack. The shack had only a wooden heater and no running water. In the country, you had to fetch water from a well with a bucket. Not to mention, you had to use the bathroom in the outhouse or in a bucket. In spite of it all, mama would keep that house clean and warm every day. She washed clothes every day and hung them on the clothesline to dry as neat as can be.

As I got older, Ike, or shall I say my daddy, would spoil me. He didn't allow me to share my toys or candy with my sisters or brothers. Many times I wanted to share with them but I couldn't because of Ike. Ike would let me stay up late but my sisters and brother had to go to bed early. Mama would be holding me in her lap and I would just stare at her because she always had big black eyes and a busted lip. Sometimes I would cry because I was scared of her. I was scared to touch my own mama because her face looked scary to me. None of us were happy in the country.

Chapter 2
The Beatings

Growing up as the baby of the family, I always thought life would be easy but I was wrong. My father was a big gambler, when it came to gambling he would spend his last dime and sometimes when he ran out of his own money he would spend mama's. If neither one of them had money he would take what was valuable out of the house and to the dice table. In addition to gambling, Ike had plenty of outside women. He spent time with so many other women that when mama would go to town she would be picked on by many of his other women. Gambling was clearly Ike's first love, if he had a good night gambling he wouldn't come home but my siblings and I always knew when he had had a bad night. We would sometimes be awakened by the sounds of screaming, the breaking of glass and the sounds of my dad's fist hitting my mom with full force.

    My oldest sister Jessica would grab us and throw us in a small, dark, and scary closet. I remember her hugging us and covering our ears, she would be shaking so hard that it could be felt by the next person. The next morning, we would all rush into the living room just to see our mothers face. There it would be all beaten up, again. It would have just begun to clear from a previous beating and then it would be all messed up again. Amazingly enough, after one of those horrible nights, my daddy Ike would be lying in bed and he would call me into the room and tell me to give him a hug. I would hug him but I had so much anger in me that when I left the room, I would cry.

No matter what, mama would still go about her daily task of cooking up a big breakfast and then cooking up a big fat dinner it would be enough to feed an army. She would do her regular washing and then ironing and then when night would fall daddy would get up, take a shower, shave and then have mom roll his hair. His hair hung long past his shoulders and he always laid out his own clothes for mom to iron. He would eat dinner with us, leave for an hour or so, then he would return home to check on momma. We would all be in bed wondering how tonight was going to be for us when he returned.

He would check each room before leaving for the night, sometimes he would come home and sometimes he wouldn't. The best sound ever was to hear him pull out of the driveway and drive off but we would still stay awake, scared. We never knew how he would return if he came home. We didn't know if he be angry or in a good mood. Many times we would just lay in the dark and talk to each other, begging God to keep him away. Many times as we laid in the dark, we would all stop breathing when we heard a car pass the house because we were scared it was daddy returning.

My sister Jessica would always say, "I wonder why he's so mean and always mad?"

My youngest brother Bubba would say, "Because he's the devil, I wish he would die."

My sister Ty would always say, "I'm running away, I hate living here and he's always mean to us and always beating on momma."

Jessica would say, "Don't talk like that you're not running away. Now all of ya'll go to sleep." We would all laugh and snuggle under each other until we fell asleep.

It's been about three days since daddy's last rage of violence and abuse towards mama. Her eyes would be less black but would still be bloodshot while the swelling was going down. At night, she would place a cold piece of steak over her eyes to help with the swelling. Sometime Ike would leave for two days and when he returned he would give mama a roll of money and act like he didn't see her black eyes and swollen lips. That money would be all it took to make her smile. It seemed that the money made mama forget about the hurtful things he had done to her. Other times, Ike would be tired from running the streets all weekend so, he would take a bath and then he would lay across the bed and with the snap of a finger he would be asleep.

    One time, mama told him she needed to run to town to pick up a few groceries. Ike mumbled "the keys are over there, on the dresser." He would then warn mama to not let grocery shopping get you into trouble today, so keep that in mind. We would be so nervous waiting to hear if momma was going to say, "ya'll come on," and wonder if he was going to reply and say, "no leave them here." This time he didn't say anything, and we were so happy to get out the house and away from him. When we arrived in town, mama would always go to this bank called *Bank First*. She would make us stay in the car and it seemed like it took her hours to come back to the car. We loved it when mama went to the bank because the bank tellers would give mama candy for us.

Before starting up the car, mama would threaten us and tell us that if we told anyone about coming to the bank then she would beat the hell out of us. She meant every word of it and by the look on her face, we knew she meant business and we wouldn't dare tell a soul. Mama would put more pressure on me because she knew that sometimes I would tell because I was daddy's girl. What she didn't know was that I didn't care for him enough to go against her wishes, I just kept my mouth shut. As long as we were in town, we would all be full of life and happiness but the closer we got to home, the more we all began to shut down. As we approached the house it would be quiet enough to hear a pen drop and sometimes I could even feel my siblings next to me shivering from fear of the next attack of abuse from my daddy. We all hated to come back to the house where that evil man lived. We never knew if he would be mad or not, when we would make it home all we could do was pray that he was asleep. As we pulled into the yard we could tell he was up waiting on us. He had the front door opened and we all began to panic, taking our time getting out the car. We were so nervous because we didn't know if he was going to jump on momma for staying away so long. We never knew exactly what to expect.

As so many times before, as soon as momma walked into the house, Ike slapped mama so hard her sunglasses flew across the room. He said, "didn't I tell you to come right back!" Momma tried to explain but he didn't give her a chance, he slapped her again. We were so nervous that we ran in our room and waited to hear him beat her. But instead he just said, "My clothes are on the bed, hurry and iron them so I can get ready." So, mama would heat the wooden stove and put the iron on it. When she finished ironing his clothes he would get dressed and lay down his rules for the night. After the rules, then, he would eat dinner and leave out the door. We were always so happy to see that car back out the driveway. We all knew that he would return shortly to check up on us so, we made sure we were all always in bed, even mama.

The next morning we were awakened by a car horn, my grandmother had bought my mom a car and we were all so happy. Now we would be able to visit our grandmother who only lived a few miles away. My grandmother said to mama, "this car is for you and those kids. I don't wanna catch that no good ass nigga driving it and I mean what I say."

We were all so happy about the car until daddy came home and said,

"Whose car parked out there?"

Then nervous as can be mama said,

"My momma bought that car so me and the kids would have a way around town."

He asked, "What kind of car is it?"

Momma said, "It's a 1969 Chevrolet."

Daddy said, it's nice but don't let that car get your ass whopped or make your head big."

You could sense the jealousy and anger coming from him. Then he said, "Enough about that damn car. Go fix me something to eat."

Before my grandmother or Madear, as we called her, left the house, she fussed at momma about her face. She asked mama, 'how long was she gonna let him beat her. Was mama gonna let him beat her until he killed her?'

Madear was screaming, "look at your damn face!!" It went through one ear and out the other with mama. It was like Madear was talking to herself.

For days after Madear bought momma the car, daddy had been having an attitude with mama. She knew that she better walk a straight line because it was just a matter of time before he would go off on her. As we all are in bed drifting off to sleep that night, we were awakened by mama's screams. We jumped up running and crying to the inside of the closet. Then came the sounds of glass breaking and mama screaming! You could hear daddy hitting mama and the sound of his fist on momma's face.

He kept yelling, "you wanna play with me bitch! You playing with the wrong one! I know that motherfucking car been moved the hood is still warm!"

Mama was screaming, "I haven't moved the car Ike! Ike, I haven't been nowhere!"

He yelled, "Bitch, stop lying, you left and went somewhere."

The hits to mama continued until the door to our room flew open. We started screaming and crying and his boots were kicking mama's face. Blood was pouring out of her nose, mouth and eyes like water. Blood was all throughout the house. Then he drug her back into to the living room and we once again heard the sound of glass breaking, the sound remains in my head to this day. It seemed like the beating was never going to stop. Ike beat mama so long that my brother Bubba ran into the living room and tried to pull him off momma. Ike pushed Bubba down and said, "Get your ass back in your room." Bubba was crying when he came back and he said, "I'm 'gonna kill him when I get big."

There was something different about this fight. Mama started fighting back and yelling, "I'm tired of you beating on me." She was fighting really hard even though Ike had power over her she still gave it all she had. She continued fighting until everything got quiet and we heard nothing but crying and moaning from her. Other than that the only sound was us crying from inside the closet. Then the door to our room flew open, it was daddy all bloody yelling, "Get yall asses out of that closet and get in the bed."

He slapped bubba behind the head four times, "saying 'lil nigga don't you ever run up on me like you wanna do something!"

Bubba just stood there huffing and puffing and crying.

Daddy said, "Do something nigga you got your chest all swollen up and shit! What you wanna do!"

Then Bubba got in bed and covered his head and cried his eyes out. When daddy left the room we all just cried and talked how much we hated this man. Then the door flew open again it was daddy! He yelled, "Tomorrow don't no one come out this room 'til I say so and I mean that!"

So, we were stuck in our rooms all day the next day. That morning mama came into our room and our hearts dropped once again there it was, her face with the busted lips and big, black swollen eyes. Mama looked at us with this funny look on her face, and it was like she was saying this is it! I'm tired! She looked at us and smiled just to let us know she was ok. Then she turned and walked out of our room, closing the door and leaving us in there all day. We didn't complain because we knew there wasn't anything she could do to help us.

Chapter 3

Leaving

As night fell, we all prepared for our baths and getting ready for bed. When we finished our baths and climbed into bed, we could smell the iron as mama was ironing daddy's clothes for tonight. She was taking her time and that really made him mad. Ike started yelling at mama and calling her all kinds of names but he finally got dressed and left the house. After all of this time, mama had learned his pattern. So, as soon as the car backed out of the driveway mama rushed into our room yelling "Get up, get up!"

She was yelling so loud. She said "Put y'all shoes on and then lay back down and cover up good cause he'll be back in a minute. Hurry up!"

After we put on our shoes, mama covered us up to our necks.

She said, "Now lay down if he comes in here, play sleep!"

I said, "Why momma?"

She said, "Be quiet and just do like I said ok!"

But what mama didn't know was that every time daddy would leave the house he would park down the road and wait for a minute, looking back at the house for any activity or lights to come on. Within minutes of mama getting us back into our bed, covered up and getting herself back into her bed, there would be the sound of keys unlocking the door. The door flew open and mama's heart almost stopped beating.

She was saying to herself, 'how the hell did he get home so early?'

Then daddy came in walking fast to mama's room, he turned on the lights and said "What the hell them lights doing on?"

Mama stayed calm and said, "Bubba's nose was bleeding but I got it stopped and he went on to bed."

Daddy said, "Oh, tell me something because you never know where I'm watching or who I got watching."

Then the sound of his 'Stacy Adams' shoes clucking on the wooden floor was getting louder as he headed toward our room. The louder the clucking got the more nervous we got. We were shaking so badly the rumbles were felt through each of our bodies and we could feel each other's hearts pounding. When he turned on the lights, we all held our breath and pretended to be sleep. He finally turned the light off and closed the door. We all took a deep breath and blew out a sigh of relief. We could hear his shoes walking from room to room then finally we heard him pick up his keys and tell mama not to turn on anymore lights or get out of bed. We then heard the door slam and the car back out of the driveway.

After he was gone mama ran into our room telling us to get up! She said "Put your jackets on hurry" She was yelling at us! Then out of nowhere, she pulled two suitcases out from under our bed already packed. She cut off all the lights and we loaded into the car. We drove very fast to my grandmother's house, we got out of the car and my grandmother was waiting at the door.

She said, "Ada! What's wrong?"

Mama said "I can't take anymore I'm tired! I gotta go! Here's my whole check, $500.00 and my food stamps. Tell Donna I will leave the car at the bus station, she can pick it up." Donna is my mom's sister and mama knew that she would be there to help my grandmother with taking care of us after she was gone.

I was crying saying, "Mama I want to go! Please don't leave me!"

Mama picked me up and said, "Mama is coming back for you ok? Mama will be back! I'm going to find us a new place to live."

I continued to say, "But, I wanna go!"

"You can't go now," Mama said.

Then my grandmother came and got me out of my mama's arms and shouted, "Go ahead before he comes Ada! I've got the kids! Hurry now!"

The trip to town is only thirty minutes, but for mama it seemed like hours. She was driving fast and looking in the rear view mirror. She was shaking so hard she could barely keep the car on the road. She was crying out of hurt, knowing that she had to leave her children and her mother behind. The whole situation was a hard pill to swallow but she made it to the bus station which was good but not good enough for my mama. She didn't know if my daddy had come home early, or if he had decided to check in. She wondered if he was on his way to town looking for her. She waited nervously, she was crying and shaking while she waited for the bus. Of all nights, the bus driver was running late. Mama kept going inside asking the clerk how much longer, wondering if he was almost there. The clerk said, "Ma'am, he should be pulling up any moment now." Mama walked back outside to the car and laid her head back on the headrest. She just knew that any moment my daddy would be pulling up looking for her, pissed. She closed her black, swollen eyes and prayed. All of a sudden she heard the horn from the bus blow, she jumped out of the car placing the keys over the visor. She ran up the steps of the bus while giving the bus driver her ticket after she boarded the bus she hurriedly went back to the very last seat. She sat down in her seat waiting nervously on the driver to board the bus, within minutes the driver came and jumped in the driver's seat. The driver began to back the bus out and mother took a deep breath. She didn't really feel safe until she saw a sign saying Chappell Hill, that sign marked her freedom. She knew she was a free woman.

Mama's body was so tired she drifted off to sleep while she was sleeping the bus made two more stops. The bus was packed to capacity and an older man was looking for a seat. The man put his hands on momma shoulders shaking her. Mama jumped out of habit, the elderly man said "excuse me ma'am, may I sit with you?"

Mama replied, "oh yes I'm sorry. I was knocked out. I am so tired."

As the elderly man got settled in his seat, the two began to talk, he asked mama if she would like a green apple because he had plenty and she said yes, thanking him.

After eating the apple, mama laid her head back and the old man said to her, "Child, you look frightened and confused. I see that you are out here running from something."

Mama asked him how he knew that but he just smiled. She told him her story and he gave her a silver coin. He told her to keep that coin with her all the time saying that it would bring her peace.

The old man had long, white hair and he was wearing a long, white shirt and sandals. When they finally made it to Houston, TX, the man helped mama down off the bus. He then hugged her and gave her another green apple. Mama bent down to get her bags and when she raised up the man was gone. To this day, mama believes that that was her guardian angel.

Mama walked her bags over to the payphones to call her niece Von. Von was shocked to receive a call from her aunt this late at night and to hear that she was at the bus station in Houston. Von rushed to get dressed and made it to the bus station in record time. She was surprised when she saw my mama's swollen black eyes and busted lips.

Von said, "Auntie you can stay with me as long as you want, I can help you get on at my job, you will have your own room and everything here. Please, auntie don't go back to the country, he will kill you, just stay here with me."

Early the next morning, mama got up and rubbed her coin the old man on the bus gave her. She made the call to the country to check up on us and Madear. We were watching television when we heard the phone ring. Madear would always sit by the phone so she could answer quickly. We were looking up in our grandmother's face when she picked up the phone, praying that it was our mama. Finally Madear said "hello baby, how are you doing?"

    We all jumped up and started fighting each other to see who could scream for mama the loudest. We wanted mama to hear us over the phone because we missed her so much but Madear told us to quiet down and we did. After we calmed down, we all got a turn to talk to mama. Mama let us know that she would be back to us real soon. After we were finished, Madear got back on the phone and asked mama to be careful. Ike had come looking for her earlier this morning. She told mama that he had knocked on the front door and that when she opened it she had a rifle in her other hand. He told Madear that he just wanted his baby but Madear told him that I would be staying right where my mama left me and to get the hell off of her land.

We then heard mama say "Don't be getting all upset with him, I don't want you getting sick."

Madear said, "I'm ok don't worry about me, just take care of you. The kids gonna be fine."

Then we each heard a final, "I love you" and those were the last words I heard my mama say for three years.

After mama got off the phone, all she could do was fall to the floor and scream out. She hurt physically and mentally. She told us later that it felt like her heart was being ripped out of her chest. She said that the pain she felt that day she wouldn't wish on her worst enemy. It was the pain of a real mother having to leave her five children and her own mother behind.

Chapter 4

Determined

It has been exactly two months since mama left us. The bruises on mama's lips are starting to heal and the swelling in her eyes have gone down tremendously. One early Wednesday morning, she got up and decided it was time for her to get a job. She went to the nursing home where her niece Von worked it was not too far from the apartments where they lived. The place was called Assisted Living Care, and mama applied for any openings that were available. The boss asked her if she could start that night as a nurse's aide working from seven to eleven. Mama quickly agreed, she was finally smiling again.

It was amazing that her new boss never asked her about what had happened to her face instead he just welcomed her with open arms. That night, as mama sat on the bus on her way to work she was thinking of her family. She was smiling on the inside because she knew that this job was the beginning of a new start for them all. She knew one day she would be able to go back to get her kids and her mother. There was a new, good spirit and feeling inside of her. When she got off the bus at the nursing home she paused before going inside and she said to herself, "This is it! This is my new start at life!

Throughout the night, mama met her coworkers and everyone was so friendly and nice. Two of the ladies even agreed to stay overnight and help train her in her new field. Within minutes, mama had caught on to most of her new duties, it was a piece of cake to her. She treated the patients like they were her very own and they really appreciated her attention.

    About three thirty in the morning, mama would take her first break of the night. She continued to meet nice friendly people. She even met a lady named Lo that lived in same apartment complex as her niece. Lo offered momma a ride to and from work that way mama didn't have to catch the bus. Lo became mama's best friend. Lo even went to talk to the landlord of the apartments about giving mama her own apartment. Lo told the landlord mamas story and about how she had to leave her five kids and her own mother behind. The landlord sent word for mama to come into the office and talk to her about filling out an application.

Two months later, mama went to talk to the landlord. She went into the office and began to share her story of abuse and how she left her five kids and mother behind in order to get away from Ike. The landlord really felt mama's pain. She gave mama a two bedroom apartment. She told mama to go ahead and move in. She told her not to worry about the deposit and that she would take care of everything else. Mama thanked the landlord so much she just couldn't thank her enough. After leaving the office mama rubbed the coin and yelled, "Thank you Lord!"

That evening before work, Lo took mama around to help centers for food, money and furniture. By that evening, mama's apartment was fully furnished except for a TV but mama wasn't too worried about a TV.

Lo had become a part of Mama's family. Mama described my daddy, Ike, to Lo just in case anything went down and Lo understood. She invited mama to a party that next weekend but Mama didn't have anything to wear. Lo went to her closet and found her the prettiest outfit with matching shoes so then Mama had no excuse but to go.

Chapter 5

Returning For Her Family

The weekend came and Lo and mama went out to the party. Lo told mama she thought that tonight would be the night that she met Mr. Right. Later that night Mama met a man by the name of Glen. They danced and exchanged addresses. Mama gave him her work number and the next day Glen called to ask her if he could take her out to eat. Glen was a very brown skinned man with a neatly trimmed afro. He was always neatly dressed and smelling good. The only thing that would turn mama off was that he was missing his left front tooth. Glen's left hand was folded in due to self-injury while cleaning his gun but he didn't let his injured hand stop from working and enjoying life. He liked to go out a lot with friends and family.

While having dinner Glen asked her mother about the marks and scars on her face to avoid the question mama asked him where he was from.

Glen replied, "I'm from Brenham."

Mama said, "I'm from Brenham too."

While getting to know each other they found out that they had things in common and that they knew a lot of the same people. It was amazing that they both knew my daddy, Ike. Mama would share with Glen the abuse she endured while with him and how she left her kids and mother.

Mama and Glen hit it off just right, and Glen started coming over and even started spending the night.

Glen started helping Mama with her bills and one day Glen surprised her with a brand new floor model TV. She was so excited, she thanked him repeatedly. At night, she would cry constantly when she was alone. Mama was really missing her family, night after night she would cry herself to sleep. One morning, Glen came over early after my mom got home from work and asked her if she was ready to go get her kids and momma? Mama was in shock.

Glen said, "Do you want to go get your family?"

Mama said, "Yes, I do but I don't know if I'm able to support them and pay my bills too."

Glen said, "Don't worry about the bills I got them, we bringing your family here."

Glen gave momma the money for a U-Haul truck, gas and food. Glen also gave momma his pistol for protection, he told her that he would take off of work to go with her if she was fearful of Ike but she refused his offer. With his pistol, Mama now had the protection that she needed.

Mama finally made the phone call to Madear to tell her that she was coming to get her and the kids. She asked her not to tell the kids that she was coming, she wanted to surprise us. The next day, late in the afternoon we were all out in the front yard playing. Madear was sitting under the China berry tree in the shade. We could see the dust coming from this big truck and we all stopped playing. We started asking who it was in that big truck flying like that toward us.

The whole time Madear knew who it was and all she did was smile. The big truck pulled up in the yard, the door opened and then finally, when all of the dust settled I saw this beautiful black woman standing beside the truck. I really didn't recognize her at first because she was so pretty and so well dressed. Then, finally, Bubba yells "That's my mama!" And everyone started running and screaming for Mama.

She was crying and we all started crying. I didn't know her by her beauty all I could remember was her beaten face. She picked me up and said, "Didn't Mama tell you she was coming back for you?" I knew that that was her, my mama. I hugged her neck so tight to let her know that, if I had my way, I was never gonna let her go away from me. Then Mama gave us orders to go get what we wanted and load it into the truck. Then she and Madear hugged and kissed, Madear was glad to see her face so smooth and pretty. So, we loaded up the U-Haul with what needed the most and headed to Houston, Texas to start a new life. When we got to Houston, Glen was waiting on us and I tell you, he was the coolest, nicest guy ever. He spoiled us rotten, and not like my daddy. Madear really liked Glen, but she had hated my Daddy, Ike.

Chapter 6
He Found Us

We have been in Houston with Mama and Glen for three, good, long years. Glen made sure we never went without, and he always made sure we had family night on the weekend. One day, he told us that he was taking us shopping for new bikes and we were all so happy. He told us to pick out whichever one we wanted regardless of the price, all he asked was that we kept our room clean and that we looked out for each other and for Madear.

As we got ready for family day, Mama was in the kitchen frying chicken and baking cakes. Glen was down on the floor playing with us, we were playing horseback riding and we were having a ball. Meanwhile,

Madear was on the couch enjoying our new color TV. Suddenly, there was a knock on the door. Mama told me to answer it and I suddenly felt like I had seen a ghost! Everyone was asking me who was at the door, but I couldn't say a word. Nothing would come out of my mouth, I was in complete shock. There stood my daddy in the doorway, I couldn't believe what I was seeing, he had found us!

    Mama pulled the door back and she couldn't believe it either. She started pushing the door with her entire weight to close it. Glen realized what was going on and who it was at the door. He jumped up and ran to the back room and returned with his long rusty rifle. Mama pulled me back into the kitchen and Glen pointed his rifle into daddy's face telling him that he better get the hell on and leave his family alone. My sisters were scared and crying and so was I, but what we didn't know was that Lo had seen him when he got out of the car and had already informed the police. Lo would always sit and look out her window all day long. The neighbors called her "Nosey Lo. " Mama always said sometimes it pays to have a nosey neighbor and she was right. Lo had noticed a strange car that kept riding through the apartment complex, a blue, late model LTD. Lo noticed that it was a black woman who was driving and a black man on the passenger side. It would always point looking back towards Mama's apartment so, Lo watched the car more and more each time it came through. Lo noticed the face of the man resembled what Mama had described to her of Daddy. So, for weeks Lo sat closer to the phone watching and waiting and today was the right day for Lo to be watching. Just as things were about to get out of hand, dozens of police pulled up. They told daddy he couldn't come back on the premises and they gave him a trespass warning. My daddy said, "That's fine I just wanted my baby."

Mama wouldn't let him take me and I didn't want to go.

My mama said, "I wanna know who else is in the car with him, and how they found me."

When Mama and the police started walking toward the car, the car started backing up. The cops ordered the driver to stop and all the cops ran over to the car pulling the driver out of the car.

Mama yelled out, "That's my sister Donna!"

The officers asked her, "Ma'am why did you tell him where your sister lived?"

Aunt Donna said, "He only wanted to see his baby."

Then momma said, "You bitch! How dirty of you!"

Mama started to run toward Aunt Donna, but the officer grabbed her and asked her to calm down. The officers made daddy get in the car and Daddy and Aunt Donna left. Mama stood still in shock that her own sister gave her away, putting her and her kids' life in danger. The good news is that that was the last time we saw or heard from my Daddy for about 8 years. As for Aunt Donna, she and Mama didn't speak for years.

In the end, the good thing about all of this drama was that Mama found a good man, she was now free and she lived to actually tell the story of the Beaten Face!

There are many women, suffering from abuse but they are hidden in silence. I wrote the book The Beaten face to touch other lives. Seeing the beating of my mother has scarred me for life, but I still live to smile and tell my story. The memories remain inside of me, but I still live a happy life. I pray that my story touches someone and helps someone come out of darkness…and live!

Resources

Domestic violence Hotline –
http://www.thehotline.org/ or
Call: 1-800-799-7233 | 1

Domestic Violence Facts

http://www.dcadv.org/domestic-violence-facts-and-faqs

Safe Horizon

http://www.safehorizon.org/page/domestic-violence-statistics--facts-52.html

Signs of Domestic Violence

http://www.webmd.com/mental-health/tc/domestic-violence-signs-of-domestic-violence

About the Author

Demeteria Kossie is a 42 year old wife, she has been married for 20 years to her wonderful husband, Charles. She is the mother of four outstanding children Tashima, 25, Vodrick, 24, Cierra, 21, and Charlesavia, 20. She also has three wonderful grandchildren. Demeteria lives in Brenham, Texas. She is committed to living a happy life as an example for her children and grandchildren. Her prayer is that her story touches someone and helps them come out of the darkness, stand strong and survive through pain.

www.ingramcontent.com/pod-product-compliance
Lightning Source LLC
Chambersburg PA
CBHW051706090426
42736CB00013B/2565